Pan the Tortoiseshell Cat's Big Adventure

The Green Grasshopper

By: Cassy M. Edwards

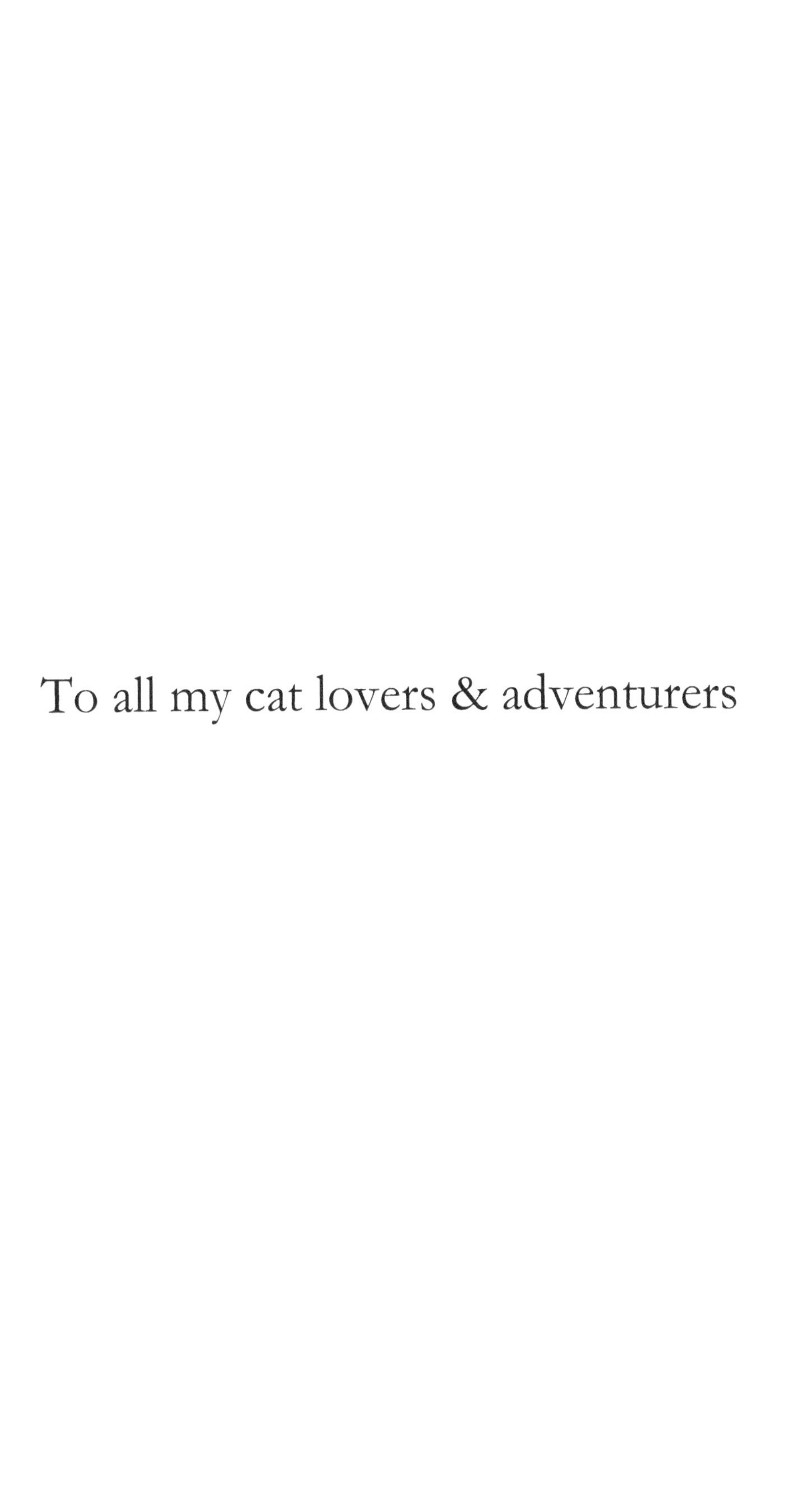

To all my cat lovers & adventurers

Once upon a time, in a cozy little cottage, there lived a tortoiseshell cat named Panther. But everyone in the neighborhood called her "Pan." Pan's backyard was her favorite place to explore, full of tall grass and colorful flowers.

One sunny morning, as Pan stretched in the warm sunlight, she noticed a cute green grasshopper named Gus hopping around. "Hello, Gus! What are you up to today?" Pan asked, her eyes shining with curiosity.

Gus, with his tiny antennae wiggling, replied, "I'm on an adventure, Pan! Would you like to join me?" Pan's whiskers twitched with excitement. "Yes, Gus! Let's go on an adventure together!"

Pan and Gus hopped through the grass, under the dappled sunlight. They discovered a magical world of miniature flowers and hidden nooks where tiny creatures lived.

They reached a sparkling pond where frogs croaked happily. Pan and Gus sat by the water, watching the ripples and giggling as tadpoles swam by.

The duo climbed the gnarled branches of an old tree, where they found a cozy nest of baby birds. Pan and Gus whispered stories to the little birds, who chirped in delight.

As they continued their journey, Pan spotted a rainbow of butterflies dancing in the air. Each fluttering wing carried a burst of color, creating a magical display.

Pan and Gus tiptoed through a field of daisies, where they encountered a family of friendly ladybugs having a picnic. The ladybugs invited them to join, and they shared tiny treats.

The duo reached a patch of soft, velvety moss. Pan lay down, and Gus hopped onto her back. They looked up at the fluffy clouds, imagining shapes in the sky.

As the sun began to set, Pan and Gus found themselves in a clearing where fireflies lit up the night. The backyard transformed into a magical realm of twinkling lights.

Gus said, "Pan, our adventure was incredible, but it's time for me to go back to my grassy home. Thank you for being my friend." Pan smiled warmly at Gus, feeling grateful for their wonderful day together.

As Gus hopped away, Pan returned to her cozy cottage. She curled up in her favorite spot, thinking about the amazing adventure she had shared with her newfound friend.

And so, the adventures of Pan, the tortoiseshell cat, continued, filled with friendship, curiosity, and the magic that could be found in the smallest corners of her backyard.

The End.